PERPETUITY
PUBLISHING

NOT ME!

NOT ME!

Convince Anyone You're Not a Problem Drinker

. . . with 145 examples

Joel L. Kruger

with Debra Bradley

PERPETUITY PUBLISHING

Published by:
Perpetuity Publishing
Tulsa, OK

ISBN: 978-0-9964646-3-5

Cover Design & Illustration: Joel L. Kruger and Debra Bradley

The author and publisher have strived to ensure that the information contained herein is accurate. Still, it may contain errors or omissions and should not be relied upon.

This publication should not be relied upon as a valid diagnostic or alcohol screening instrument or when deciding whether to seek **any** treatment. The author and publisher cannot provide any professional advice. Please consult the appropriate healthcare provider to address your concerns.

Any reference to names, characters, businesses, organizations, places, events, and incidents is fictitious or used fictitiously. Any resemblance to actual persons, living or dead, events, or locales is entirely coincidental.

Cataloging-in-publication data is on file with the Library of Congress.

First Edition
First Printing
Printed in the United States of America.

THIS BOOK IS DEDICATED
to the millions of suffering
alcoholics in denial
and
the many more
affected by them.

ACKNOWLEDGMENTS

A JOKE IS always funnier the first time it's heard than the tenth. This reality made it challenging to create and review revisions. So, I have special admiration and gratitude for my editors, Pamala Sipes and Debra Bradley, who endured countless revisions as the punchlines lost their punch. Pamala consistently paid attention to details. Debra contributed significantly by suggesting I change the original format from a written diagnostic multiple-choice test to its current format, making it more engaging and humorous. She communicated much to me through her authentic and contagious laughter—her words became less necessary. Their talents and patience are outstanding.

I sincerely appreciate the many readers and reviewers who provided invaluable feedback that helped shape this book over the past ten years.

Much of the information in this book came from years of listening to thousands of drinking alcoholics deny their alcoholism and thousands of sober alcoholics discuss their experiences. I'm eternally grateful to all who, by sharing their experience, strength, and hope, collectively gave me the ability to put this in writing rather than slurring it from a bar stool.

Author's Note

LAUGHTER CAN BE the best medicine. This is a satirical diagnostic exam that highlights with exaggerated humor the absurd ways alcoholics justify and rationalize their drinking to remain deep in denial. It humorously exposes the signs and symptoms of alcoholism by using many of the actual diagnostic questions from the best-selling book *Light Reflections Into THE DARKNESS OF DENIAL . . . and the alcoholic mind*, written by the same author as this book.

Sober alcoholics in recovery can often laugh at themselves and their past behavior. This humor *is* essential for healthy, long-term sobriety and is not meant to be insensitive or disrespectful. Most sober alcoholics are keenly aware of the pain, suffering, and trauma their drinking has caused others who *may* still harbor resentment.

Still, without this humorous attitude, the sober alcoholic remains chained to the past, and their guilt and self-loathing will likely reach a crescendo so painful and debilitating that their journey for relief can be deadly—or worse—relapsing and living the rest of their shortened lives hopelessly *demoralized*.

—

IF YOU OR a loved one is suffering from or affected by alcoholism, there are many organizations and people ready to help, and change is much easier than you might think.

The last pages of this book list helpful contact information. It just requires the willingness to reach out to change one's life by pressing a few phone buttons.

The Only Chapter

—

Sue, Jim, and John

THIS IS ABOUT Sue and Jim, who have been married for seven years. They have an eight-year-old daughter and a newborn baby. Sue has been struggling with Jim's drinking even though Jim doesn't think he has a drinking problem.

Sue decides to talk to someone about it. She finds herself sitting on a couch, meeting with John Hansen, a therapist who comes highly recommended to couples dealing with a drinking problem.

"So, Sue, what brings you here today?" John asks while adjusting his perfectly round, wire-rimmed glasses like a therapist would.

"It's my husband, Jim," she begins with a heavy sigh. "He has a drinking problem but claims the only drinking problem he has is me ruining his drinking. His drinking is way out of control, but he sluffs it off by making jokes about it."

John leans in. "Interesting. Denies it with humor. Can you give me an example?"

"Sure, I can. Just last night, he drank half a bottle of whiskey, and when I asked him about it, he swore it must have been the cat."

John hides a smile. "The cat? How imaginative."

"Imaginative? Try delusional! The cat is on a strict diet of tuna and salmon and doesn't drink."

Their session continues, with Sue recounting some of Jim's actions. "His denial has become absurd. Last night, when I saw him drinking, I asked him what was in the glass, and he said it was apple juice that looks like whiskey."

John nods with the calmness of a man who's heard it all but wishes he hadn't. "Go on."

The minutes pass with tales of Jim's drinking. "It's crazy! He was arrested for public drunk when in court for a DUI, uses the Braille bumps on the road to drive, started a class on how to drive better drunk, brags about how well he holds his liquor, decorates our house with Crown Royal bags, dresses our baby in them, dressed our cat to look like King Crown Royal, rarely goes anywhere unless alcohol is there, has me carry his flasks in a big, ugly purse that he makes me use, and I could go on and on and on.

John asks, "How do you feel about this, Sue?"

"How do I feel? If it doesn't end, I might start believing I'm the one with a problem."

John comments, "Well, we know that you have at least one problem, and that's Jim's drinking. Perhaps it's time to consider an intervention. I'd like to visit with Jim if you think he'd be willing to see me."

"He probably will if he can blame everything on me. But who knows, I'll see."

The next week, Jim arrives to meet with John.

AFTER INTRODUCTIONS, JOHN asks Jim, "Why do you think you're here?"

"Because my wife, Sue, has a drinking problem."

"You think Sue has a drinking problem?"

"Of course I do! She has a problem with my drinking, so isn't that a drinking problem?"

"Cute! But if we can be serious for a moment, do you think there's any validity to her concerns, or is she just completely off-base?"

"She's completely off-base. Now, I'll admit that, at times, my drinking may get a little out of hand. But hey, I'm human and make mistakes every so often. Who doesn't? But she uses my drinking to blame everything that's wrong with her and the world. I hope you can help her."

"Well, would you be willing to explore whether there's any reality to her concerns? That is, whether you might have a drinking problem?"

"You bet! Maybe this will finally calm her down, but who knows? By the way, here's a notarized certificate stating that I don't have a drinking problem."

"Thanks, Jim. So, are you willing to answer some questions honestly? If not, this is just a waste of time!"

"Ask me whatever you want and as many questions as you want—I'm more than willing!"

THE FOLLOWING ARE Jim's answers to John's questions during this session.

1. Jim, have you ever wondered if you might have a drinking problem?

Well, John, once I was in a dry county, and I couldn't find any alcohol, none! I had to find a bootlegger. So, since I had a problem getting a drink, I guess you can call that a drinking problem. But I didn't *wonder* if I had one; I knew I did.

2. Would you be willing to go one year without a drink—starting now?

Why would I do that? That's like me asking you if you'd be willing to go one year without your smartphone—starting now! Get what I'm saying?

3. Where do you usually keep your alcohol?

I keep a bottle in my trunk, but I never plan on taking it anywhere. No one else knows it's there, and I'm the only one with the key. Great idea, isn't it? I also keep one in my toolbox and one in the tank of my commode, which saves water, except when I flush twice.

4. Your wife mentioned that after you have a few, you can't speak clearly enough for people to understand you. Any truth to that?

That's just cold of her. She knows I have a disorder that causes my tongue to swell and my mouth to shrink when I drink more than a couple. And she knows there's no cure.

5. Have you ever put one foot on the floor to stop the bed from spinning after drinking too much? If so, did it work?

Yes, it slowed it down, but both feet on the floor worked better. When the bed spins one way, then quickly reverses and spins the other way, or my room spins one way while my bed spins the other way, faster and faster, I find that quickly getting out of the spinning bed and room and kneeling before a mass of porcelain works best. And if that's too uncomfortable, I just take off my clothes and lay in a cold bathtub without any water, which always slows down the spinning.

> 6. Do you have any items with a beer or liquor logo imprinted?

I'm glad you asked. I do have a bed-spread hand-quilted with Crown Royal bags. I wish it were quilted with bags of different sizes, but I'm not complaining. And I'm so excited! I heard an article about me and my spread might be in a popular magazine. I think it's called *Psychology Today!* If it makes it in there, I'll give you my autograph. By the way, here's a picture of it. Who knows, maybe it'll make the cover.

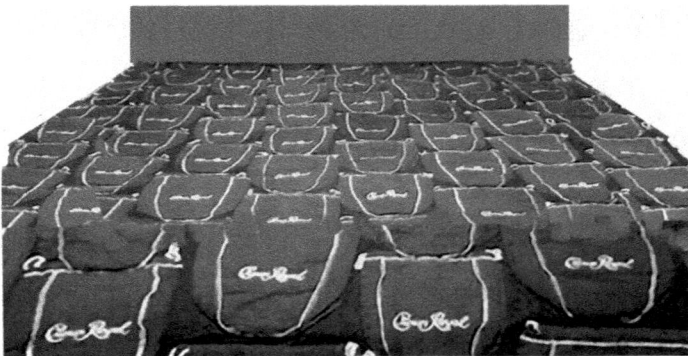

7. Have you ever drunk from a liquor bottle?

Sure! I figure it's okay because people drink out of beer bottles all the time without anyone getting their panties in a twist. And it saves on washing dishes. But when I did it in public, I wrapped it in a brown paper sack so no one knew what it was. It's one of those things that most people do all the time, but they don't talk about it, like peeing in the shower, if you know what I mean.

8. Is it true that once, after drinking a few, you proclaimed, "One person can make a difference," and you formed a group called "Mad Drinkers Against Madd Mothers?"

Absolutely not. That would be in bad taste. Now, I'll admit that once, when I was half-tanked, I might have said I was forming a group called that, but I ended up calling it "Drunk Drivers Have Rights, Too." It never caught on, and can you believe I still get flack for that?

9. Have you ever been the subject of an intervention?

Sure, I have! Sue does about four a year, so I just keep the folding chairs open. But these aren't actual interventions. They're just Sue's way of keeping in touch with family and friends who feel forced to attend while she *tries* to keep it alcohol-free. So, most of us just have a little tailgate party, which usually turns out to be not so little when neighbors show up with cases of beer and other stuff—if you know what I mean. I just put up with it!

10. Do you know where every liquor store is within five miles of your home?

Sure, doesn't everyone? And I don't know if I've mentioned it, but I am strongly against driving drunk. That's why I try not to drive more than three miles when I've been drinking. Five miles is my limit because it's a bit far when I'm drunk.

11. Do you have a favorite liquor store, or do you alternate between different ones?

I go to about five different ones, but it's not because I don't want the clerks to get the wrong idea and think I have a problem. I just prefer the ones that greet me with: "Good *morning*, Jim, glad to see you again." The others are okay, but they say things like, "Good thing I got here early, so you didn't have to wait even longer." I don't need their comments—if you know what I mean.

12. Please examine this image and tell me what you see. There are no wrong answers.

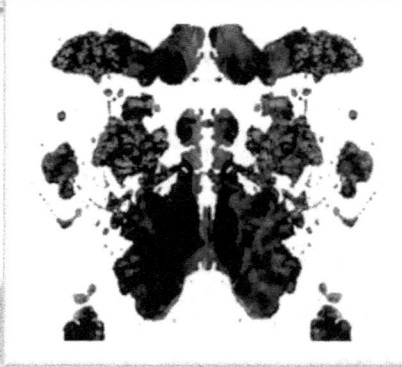

I don't know what showing me an inkblot of a Sippy cup filled with whiskey on the rocks surrounded by quacking ducks could possibly tell you. Wait a minute . . . maybe it's two people holding umbrellas leaning on a bar, drinking shots. Or it could be an intervention going bad with Sue throwing a temper tantrum. So, since there's no wrong answer, I got this right! I like these questions; let's do more like these.

13. After two drinks, do you usually continue drinking instead of eating?

Now you sound like my mother. Don't worry, I won't starve. I take my one-a-day gummy vitamin *twice* a day—usually.

And yes, I'm financially responsible. I adjusted my budget to reflect my actual spending by decreasing my food and increasing my alcohol expenses. So now, I'm living within my budget—something Sue and others should try doing. Still, I'm not sure what all this has to do with my drinking, but you asked, and I answered.

14. Have you ever set a limit on the number of drinks you planned to have? If so, did you exceed that limit?

Yes—No. You see, I'm flexible, and I'm even more flexible after drinking a couple, so I use a method I proudly developed called *flexi-limit*. I set a new limit after each drink. This way, I never exceed my limit. And if Sue is around, it doesn't matter because, after a few drinks, she's the only one counting.

I think that's much better than those who say, "No thanks. I've had enough." They obviously have a drinking problem if they have to stop at two.

15. Have you noticed you drink more than you once did to get the same effect?

Yeah, you notice that, too? I think the distilleries are watering down their liquor or doing something else to sell more. I'm glad someone else sees it because I thought it was just me.

16. What does sobering up mean to you?

That always confuses me. Why don't they call it "sobering down?" It's like we say, "calm down," not "calm up." Anyway, to me, it means drinking beer ... mostly.

17. I heard you once googled "safe recipe for a rubbing alcohol martini." Is that true?

How do you know this? Is Google rereleasing my private information? Whatever. But yeah, I was just in a bind, I mean, not in a bind, but you know what I mean, I was just curious. I ended up not trying it, which proves I don't have a drinking problem.

> **_DISCLAIMER:_** This does not allege Google releases private data or does anything wrong or everything right.

> **_SERIOUS WARNING:_** Drinking rubbing alcohol is never safe and will likely kill or seriously and permanently injure you.

18. Your wife, Sue, mentioned that you bought everyone a round of drinks at your neighborhood bar even though you really couldn't afford it then. Any truth to that?

She mentioned that, did she? Well, yes, it's true, and it caused me to request an extension on my electric bill, which was denied.

She wasn't very happy about it, so she ran off with the kids to her parents. Since she left me all alone without electricity in my dark, hot house, I returned to the bar to cool off, expecting the people I bought drinks for to buy me drinks. Nope! So, I was forced to spend the rest of the money I'd been saving for my electric bill, which kept us without power even longer.

So that tells you I have a *giving* problem, not a *drinking* problem.

19. Jim, I heard that the time you were without power was on Valentine's Day, and after an argument with Sue about the electric bill, you ended up drinking all alone with your sick, unbathed dog Whiskey in a dim, candlelit room. And I see you proudly proclaimed in a group text that "No one is worthy of me." Any comment?

That's just wrong. See how disturbed Sue must be to send you that text? Please help her! And no, I asked, "Anyone up to drinking whiskey with me?" I spoke that text, but my phone got it wrong, and I sent it before I noticed. And how could I have been "all alone" if I was with Whiskey?

20. Did you once select flooring by putting your face against it to evaluate the pass-out comfort?

What hasn't she told you? I'll let you know right now that it was her idea. She said I should look for comfy flooring to pass out on, and I thought she finally cared. But it's not as bad as it sounds; I stepped off to the side when I did it so no one could see me. I have manners, you know, even when I'm drinking.

21. Has anyone ever invited you to an AA meeting?

Only those alcoholics who are in AA. And the only reason they did is because they don't want me drinking since they can't drink.

22. So, did you consider attending an AA meeting after you were invited?

Well, I learned that AA is either for alcoholics who don't drink and want to stay sober or alcoholics who drink and want to stop. Strike one: I'm not an alcoholic. Strike two: I drink. Strike three: I don't want to stop. So, I figured I struck out, right?

23. So, you decided not to attend?

Well, I finally went to support a friend and saw people who seemed happy and content but 'claimed' they didn't drink. And get this, there was this alcoholic— *claiming* he'd been sober for 30 years —who said, "Whoever woke up the earliest today has the most sobriety." What kind of drunk math is that? Something about all of that I just didn't trust.

Still, I wanted something out of that wasted hour, so I did these 12 steps they harped about, and by the end of the meeting, I had them down per-fectly. That's a big deal because people said they worked on them their whole lives but never got them perfect. Still, I never got the promises they promised me. Who knows? I might still get them someday, but I'm not holding my breath waiting.

24. I see the court finally ordered you to attend AA. How did that work?

Well, I'll tell you how it works. They claim they have no dues or fees but pass a basket collecting "contributions." So it cost me two bucks to get my attendance sheet signed.

And they say they have no rules, but they have this 4 x 7-foot banner on the wall with 12 rules in big letters. One rule is that you need to have a desire to stop drinking to be there. And they introduce themselves as alcoholics. Well, as I said, since I don't have a desire to stop drinking and I'm not an alcoholic, I didn't feel right being there. So I hit it off with another court-ordered person, and we signed each other's attendance sheet for free while drinking at the bar next door. Wasn't that a great idea?

> 25. Have you ever said or done anything while drinking that you later regretted?

I've done things I wouldn't have regretted, but since Sue did, she made sure I regretted it. Does that count?

But I would say no because that's one good thing I got out of that AA meeting. They promised that if I paid two bucks, I "wouldn't regret the past." I'm serious. They even put these promises on a sign that is titled in big letters, "THE PROMISES," hung next to the huge banner listing all the rules they don't have.

26. Have you ever drunk while taking medicine that had this warning label on it?

> **Warning:** Taking this medicine with alcohol may intensify the effect and may lessen your ability to drive or perform hazardous tasks.

Once I saw a warning like that and shouted: "Let's Party!" Just kidding. Seriously, though, I usually don't read warnings. But once, I read one like that and was curious, so I doubled the dose to check if the warning label was accurate. It's spot-on, alright. But you need to understand that I drive and perform hazardous tasks better when I drink and take drugs—prescribed, that is.

27. I've also heard you have *new* Crown Royal drapes. Is there any truth to that?

Yes, they even look better than the old ones we replaced because Sue cut them into little pieces with scissors. I'm always really proud of how speechless people are when they see them and take pictures. Here's a picture.

Still, I'm not sure what my decorating has to do with my drinking.

28. Sue mentioned that your local bar calls to check on you if they haven't seen you in a few days. Any truth to that?

Nope, I've never been away for a few days. But they'll text if they haven't seen me for a day or two. If I had a drinking problem, I doubt they'd miss me that much to check on me, right?

29. Have you ever taken Nyquil®
when you weren't sick?

Well, I remember thinking about it when I wasn't sick, but by the time I quit thinking about it, I was feeling flu-like symptoms. And it had nothing to do with the alcohol in it. So, I guess the answer is no.

> 30. Has anyone ever said, "Don't you think you've had enough?" If so, what did you say?

Well, of course, Sue has when she's so miserable that she wants me to feel miserable. So, since I'm learning to set healthy boundaries, I say something like, "No, but I've had enough of you!" Other times, I ignore her and quickly drink more to teach her a lesson. It seems to work because she either gets quiet, looks down, and acts ashamed, or throws one of her tantrums and takes off, which is even better.

31. Have you carried a flask of alcohol in the past year?

Not usually, because I keep one or two in Sue's purse. I bought her a huge one that's so beautiful people are always commenting about it. But if she's not with me, I carry a bottle or two in my trunk. Now, I'll admit I may carry a flask if I'm alone and away from my car, but that's the only time . . . usually.

32. Will you examine this picture and tell me how many legs the elephant has?

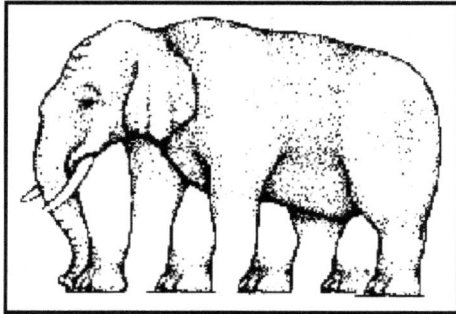

This is obviously a sobriety test. I don't know how the elephant changes the number of its legs, but I counted between four and eight. And I promise I only had one shot before this session. And I'm still not wearing the right glasses, but I can tell you it has one . . . or maybe two trunks. I'd rather touch the tip of my nose with my eyes closed while standing on one leg and reciting the alphabet backward than try to figure this out.

33. Are you ever asked to be the designated driver?

Not as often as I should be. But I'm a great choice because I'm a good driver when I've been drinking since I've had a lot of practice.

34. Have you ever seen three center lines when drinking and driving? If so, what did you do?

I quickly used a technique I thought of called "cross-eyed" mode. Then, I saw only one blurry line.

And the times I couldn't even see one blurry line, I used the rumbling of the Braille bumps on the centerline and the shoulder to nudge me back into my lane. But on roads without Braille bumps, the curb bumps me back into my lane—like bumper cars. It works great when I'm driving with one eye closed to see better—if you know what I mean. That's why they're there, so I might as well use them, right?

35. Has anyone ever hidden your car keys after you've been drinking?

Of course, Sue has, but she's just a control freak. So, I gave her a copy of my key to hide, and I kept the original. You should see her face when I've had a couple, start the car, and yell "ha-ha" out the window as I drive off. It's hilarious. But on a more serious note, what does that have to do with a drinking problem?

36. During an average month, how often do you drink and drive?

As I've said, I'm very much against drunk driving, but my Uber account was suspended for what they called "inappropriate conduct," so I have no choice but to drive after I've been drinking at times. But know this: The only time I do is when I need to get somewhere.

37. I heard you started a class called *How Not To Get Caught Driving Drunk*. Any truth to that?

Not much truth to it. It was called *How to Drive Better Drunk*, but it never got off the ground. It's a great idea. Just think of all the lives it could save.

Here are three of my tips: First, the next time you're driving drunk, open both eyes and focus about 300 feet in front of you instead of looking with one eye closed just beyond the hood, as most drunk drivers do. Second, get a sign that says: **STUDENT DRIVER.** And third, turn on your flashers and drive slower.

And if you do all three at once, you'll be amazed at how well it works. It's worked every time for me except for three. And three out of . . . thousands of times are pretty good odds, wouldn't you say?

38. I see you were recently charged with a third DUI. Is there anything you'd like to say about it?

Why say "third" DUI instead of your *last* DUI? It sounds worse than it really is. Anyway, I was at the wrong place at the wrong time. The cop said I was repeatedly crossing the center line, but here's the real deal. To be safe, I was preparing to pass the drunk driver in front of me, so I kept veering over the line to see when it was safe to pass. Had it not been for that drunk driver in front of me, I wouldn't have been arrested for DUI.

> **39. I see that you were later arrested for public drunk while in court for a DUI. Any comments?**

Wow! Nothing gets past you, does it? I'd love to comment, but my lawyer advised me not to discuss any pending legal matters.

But, come on, it's always so stressful going to court for a DUI, so I drank a few to take the edge off. The judge thought I was disruptive, so he asked two deputies to cuff and escort me to the Drunk Tank. But I wasn't *really* arrested because I was released after a few hours. That's all—no biggie. I hope you don't think that shows I have a drinking problem.

40. I see that at your last DUI, the court ordered a breathalyzer interlock device installed in your car. How did that go?

Great! We have two cars, so I just switched cars with Sue, who rarely drinks. And when she was in one of her moods and wouldn't let me drive her car to get somewhere like the grocery or liquor store, I brought my 8-year-old daughter to blow in it. I told her it was a game and gave her candy when she blew hard enough to start the car and keep it going. It was so cute. And when she wasn't with me, I paid the neighbor kid to ride with me. So, to answer your question, Sue made it a little inconvenient, but it wasn't that big of a deal.

41. Jim, can you explain why you missed this question on your last DUI school test?

DUI School Exam

8. What should you do if you've been drinking and need to go somewhere?
   a) Don't drink and drive
   b) Learn to drive drunk
   c) Let someone less drunk drive
   d) Drink five cups of strong coffee
   e) Obey traffic laws and drive carefully
   f) All the above

I picked "f) All the above." I still think I got it right. Think about it. Say I *need* to get somewhere like urgent care when I've been drinking, then I have to drive. And, if I've learned to drive drunk, wouldn't that be safer? And if I'm in a bind, shouldn't someone less drunk drive? And strong coffee can't hurt, right? And shouldn't I obey traffic laws and drive carefully, especially when I've been drinking? I still can't believe they marked it wrong!

42. I see here that you caused a breath-alyzer to malfunction because you were too drunk for it to register.

Oh, here we go again. You know how many times I've had to explain this. Okay, I'm not taking the blame for breaking it; it was defective, so it means nothing about my drinking.

43. Do you control your drinking? If so, how?

Sure, I control my drinking by *usually* not ordering more than one drink at a time and only drinking one at a time. Another way I control it is by not taking a shot before every drink but instead before every other drink. And then I've got Sue, always trying to control my drinking for me. I can go on and on, but I'm sure you can see my drinking is controlled.

44. Can you hold your liquor better now than three years ago?

Of course, I can. I've had three more years of practice!

45. After two drinks, do you usually continue drinking instead of eating?

Now you sound like my mother. Don't worry, I won't starve. I take my one-a-day gummy vitamin *twice* a day—usually.

And yes, I'm financially responsible. I adjusted my budget to reflect my actual spending by decreasing my food and increasing my alcohol expenses. So now, I'm living within my budget— something Sue and others should try doing. Still, I'm not sure what all this has to do with my drinking, but you asked, and I answered.

46. Does your drinking ever interfere with your work?

Since you promised that my boss can't ever find out my answers, the answer is *no*. You see, I drink less when I'm working, so my work interferes with my drinking more than drinking interferes with my work.

47. Do people think you're a happy, sad, mean, obnoxious, funny, or loving drunk?

I really don't know what people think of me when I'm drunk if they think anything. But I know I'm happy, funny, and loving when drunk—never mean or obnoxious!

Now once, when I was pulled over, I was sad and cried, which got me a ride home instead of jail.

By the way, I bet Sue didn't tell you that before that nice trooper took me home, he called her to get me, and she said, "Take him straight to jail where he belongs!"

48. Is it true that after having a few, you once decided to buy a pool table instead of paying your taxes?

Sue's never gotten over this. The answer is *no*! You see, I intended to pay my taxes instead of buying the pool table. Then, I decided that a few drinks would help calm me down and help me think more clearly. And I was right because after drinking a few, I asked myself if I would enjoy a pool table more than paying taxes. The answer came quickly—buy the pool table *and* pay my taxes over time. So, now I'm enjoying the pool table and paying my taxes with an interest rate less than on a pool table loan. It was a wise choice, even if she didn't think so. This way, everyone wins! More proof that drinking helps me think more clearly.

49. Please examine this image and tell me what you see. No wrong answer.

Here goes. Another sobriety test? Alright, give me a minute to concentrate. Okay, I see ... two ... no ... three blurry black boxes ... no, now there's only one ... Are we supposed to be sober when we take this test? Wait a minute ... I see a blackout. Or is it a white square painted black? It might be a rectangle, but I'd need to measure it to tell you for sure. Another right answer! Yes!

50. Is it true that once your blood donation was rejected because it had too much alcohol in it?

You've got to be kidding me. That's funny! You've got to take whatever Sue says with a grain of salt. What happened was I returned home after giving blood, and Sue smarts off with, "I can't believe they took your blood. Anybody they give it to is going to get drunk." So, I told her not to worry because they put a warning label on it that said, "This blood must not be given to anyone under 21 years of age." Just some sarcastic humor—if you know what I mean.

51. Do you ever try to delay drinking after you first think about it when you have access to it?

No, I've never thought about doing that. Why would I? That's like me asking, "Do you ever delay peeing after you first think about it when you have access to a bathroom?" I must say, some of your questions are just silly.

52. Have you ever said or thought that you hold your liquor well?

I usually don't brag because that's not how I was raised. But sometimes I do if I've got something to really brag about. And let's face it, holding my liquor better than most *is* something to brag about. So, since I can drink a lot more than most without stumbling around drunk, doesn't that prove right there that I don't have a drinking problem?

53. What does this phrase mean to you? There is no wrong answer.
"Too much of anything is not enough of nothing."

I'm not saying I don't know, but your question makes me thirsty—if you know what I mean. Okay, I think I got it. It means I shouldn't listen to my wife so much, or try drinking slower, or drink a glass of water between drinks. Oh, wait! It means my drinks have too much water and not enough whiskey. Or maybe it means I drink too much and should drink less . . . no, that wouldn't make sense. Okay, you got me again; it means nothing; it's a trick question! Another right answer!

54. Please examine this image and state what you see. Again, no wrong answer.

I like these questions. Okay, I see a few things. I see two aliens looking at each other, starting to kiss. Or maybe it's a bong. Or it could be a pier post with the sun rising or setting over the sea. Or perhaps it's some eclipse or a broken spotlight. Another right answer, so give me a star!

55. If you've heard "last call" announced in the past year, were you surprised by how quickly the time passed?

You, too? I'm glad I'm not the only one. I really don't know how that happens. I go in for a couple of beers after work when it's daylight; the next minute, it's two in the morning. I'm not one of those conspiracy guys, but I think they either put something in the drinks or pump something in the air because when Sue's at home waiting for me, she doesn't think the time flies by that quickly.

> 56. I heard that after a night of heavy drinking, the first thing you do upon awakening is look at your phone to see who you called or texted. Is that true?

You've got to be kidding me. It's Sue who looks at my phone when she first wakes up to see who I called or texted. And I doubt she told you she uses face recognition to unlock my phone by holding it in front of my face while I'm sleeping. Isn't that crazy? I sure hope you can help her.

Now, I'll admit that *sometimes*, I've looked to see who I called or texted so I could do whatever I needed to fix things. But I bet people with a drinking problem don't even bother to do that.

57. Were you so drunk in the past year that you slurred this text?

Hey Sandy i mean ah damn Sue...... Sorry?...i love you sooooo mush and be home soon. Not drinking.!!...I not have 2 or 1 drop of lic her—pr pr promise

Is she really sending you more old texts? As I said, my phone's speech-to-text feature isn't that good, especially when I'm in a loud place. So, I tried editing it using my big thumbs without glasses. I hope you don't think a couple of texting mistakes are enough to be called an alcoholic. I feel like you're scraping the bottom of your question barrel—if you know what I mean.

58. After having a few and feeling great, do you ever quickly drink more to feel even better?

Who doesn't want to feel better? I'll admit that when I'm feeling great, I'll keep drinking to keep feeling great, but I don't know about "quickly." I'll also admit that sometimes, to keep feeling great, I may miscalculate, drink more than I need to, and then I'll feel "even better." But hey, I'm human. So, I might have a human problem but not a drinking problem.

59. Have you ever missed an important event because of drinking?

Well, I don't go to school events or other important events when I've been drinking a lot, if that's what you mean.

Also, after I thought about it, I decided the missed events weren't all that important, despite what Sue thinks. So, the answer is *no*.

> 60. Does any of your clothing, such as caps, T-shirts, sweatshirts, jackets, etc., have a beer or liquor logo?

I have a T-shirt, a cap, and a sweatshirt with beer logos. But no liquor logos, except for my Crown Royal jump-suit. I'm told I look cute in it even though Sue doesn't think so—like a walking Crown Royal bag. And my 8-year-old daughter uses a Crown Royal bag as a purse; it's adorable! And I dress our baby in them. Does that mean they have drinking problems? Oh, here's a picture of our baby. Isn't he cute?

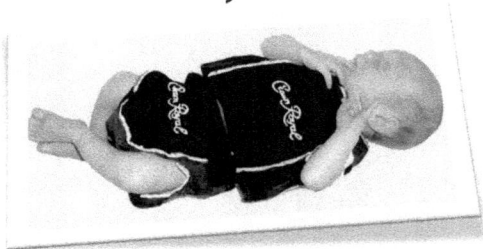

Oh, did Sue mention the time she took scissors and cut over 100 bags she found into dime-sized pieces?

61. You mentioned earlier you're so relieved no one harasses you about
drinking anymore and said it's
probably because they don't care
anymore. What did you mean?

Well, I didn't mean they don't care about *me* anymore. I was saying they don't care about my *drinking* anymore, except for Sue, of course. And I'm relieved that they don't because it means they finally get that Sue, not my drinking, is the problem. I sure hope Sue gets it one of these days.

62. Your wife mentioned that you refused to pay your bar tab the last time you went to Happy Hour. Is that true?

You bet! It's deceptive advertising. I drank five drinks during one "happy hour" but wasn't very happy. Come on, all I'm saying is don't deceive me by calling it "Happy Hour" without making me happy, so I refused to pay. Plus, it's always longer than an hour. Don't know what this has to do with my drinking, but . . .

> 63. When deciding whether to attend an event, do you check to see if alcohol will be served?

Yes, all I really want to know is if I need to bring my own. And, if I'm the only one drinking, how much fun can that be? I might as well go to an AA meeting or church or someplace like that—if you know what I mean.

64. Do you usually have a few at home before going to a party or the bar?

Since I hold my liquor so well, I usually drink before a party so people don't think I'm rude drinking all the liquor or the bartender doesn't think I'm drinking too much.

65. Have you ever promised yourself or anyone you would never drink again?

I know Sue thinks I promised that, but I didn't because I had my fingers crossed behind my back. Plus, everyone has said that a time or two when they drank too much, but they always drink again. That's why I'm outraged every time she says I broke my promise to stop drinking. Come on, I can't break a promise I never made. So, I'll admit to being a cross-fingerer, but at least I'm not a cross-dresser. I should get another star for that!

66. Do you ever avoid disclosing the time of day you start drinking?

Only with Sue. If I told her, I would have to explain daylight-saving time in detail, which confuses her when I explain that although I'm drinking at an earlier time, I'm actually drinking later than she thinks. She has a hard time understanding that.

67. Have you ever tried acting sober to keep anyone from knowing you had been drinking?

Funny you say "acting" because I took an acting class for that very purpose. The session was on how to act drunk, so I just learned how to act the opposite. I've become so good at it that I started my own class called "How to Act Sober." But I only act sober when I need to, like when I'm in court, at work, at a job interview, pulled over, or with Sue.

68. Do you think beer is a breakfast drink?

It is if you drop a raw egg in a beer and drink it for breakfast. Or if you pour a little tomato juice in one with a pinch of salt, it's good stuff to start the day. But even if you don't put anything in it, it's really an anytime drink, 24-7.

> 69. Upon awakening after a night of drinking, have you ever been surprised to see who was in your bed? If so, what happened?

These days, I'm quite surprised if I see Sue in my bed.

And, back in the day, I remember some women were offended if they thought they knew me well enough to be in my bed, but I didn't remember them. So, I learned to pretend I was sleeping and just let things happen naturally, although I no longer have to worry about that.

Oh, and once, just before I got married, I was much more pleasantly surprised than usual, but it didn't go very well because I was a little too introductory—if you know what I mean.

70. I've heard that when you drink, you occasionally come up missing. Any truth to that?

Here we go again. No, I never come up missing! Even when Sue can't find me, I always know where to find me . . . or almost always.

71. Sue mentioned that you once said that if you quit drinking, you wouldn't have anything or anyone to blame for your mistakes. True?

Well, I was half joking, but isn't it true? Like when I make a mistake after drinking, I can say, "Sorry, I never would've done that sober." Or, if I miss an easy shot when shooting pool, I say, "I've obviously had a bit to drink." It comes in really handy at times.

One thing your questions do is remind me about all the benefits of drinking.

72. Have your friends or family *ever* complained about your drinking? If so, what did you say?

Well, of course. I wouldn't be here if Sue never complained, right? Anyway, I ignored her, drank more, and demanded she get counseling immediately, which I'm happy she's done.

73. Have you ever celebrated any period of sobriety?

That's a funny question—celebrate and sobriety in the same sentence. There's nothing about being sober I could ever imagine celebrating. And even if I wanted to, how could I if I didn't drink? Think about it!

74. Look at this image and tell me what you see.

What? Is this the third sobriety test? I'd rather try balancing on one leg while in quicksand.

Okay, I'm still not wearing the right glasses, but I'll do my best. The longer I stare at it, it changes from an older woman looking to the left to a younger woman facing away, and I didn't drink that much before this test. Wait a minute . . . it's Sue switching between giving me the silent treatment and then preparing to go crazy on me again. Yeah, that's it!

75. Do you ever have hangovers? If so, how do you handle them?

Who hasn't? But I've got that down, too! It's easy. The first thing I do is get away from Sue because she uses my hangovers to torture me. Next, I just knock down shots until one stays down, then I drink two more, and . . . WALA! You ought to try it if you haven't.

76. Do you ever monitor how much you drink, or do you freely drink as much as you want whenever you want?

I didn't know I could drink "freely." Where can I drink as much as I want for free?

77. Have you ever resisted getting help with your drinking out of fear that someone might think you have a drinking problem?

Why would I get help with a drinking problem I don't have? See what I'm saying?

Besides that, I'm not afraid of people thinking I have a drinking problem because plenty of people who listen to Sue think I do. But I think you're figuring out that I don't.

78. Do you have times when you've been drinking that you don't remember, called blackouts?

How can I remember the times I don't remember? So, I really don't remember. But every so often, I'll have brownouts; does that count? You know, a time I can't remember until Sue tries to remind me about a time that never happened the way she remembers it.

79. Do you ignore comments people make about your drinking?

I don't ignore *all* the comments, just the ones Sue and the people who believe her make. For example, I wouldn't ignore a comment like, "It looks like you could use a couple; I'm buying!"

80. Has a bartender ever placed your next drink in front of you before you finished the last one without you asking for it?

Sure! We have an understanding, and I tip well—when I tip. But wouldn't that tell you more about the bartender than about me? I must say that some of your questions are better than others.

81. When making decisions, do you think about how your decision will affect your drinking?

To be honest, I think more about how Sue's decisions will affect my drinking because she's always trying to control it. So, if anything, I think more about how my decisions will affect Sue's decisions.

82. Have you ever thought, "If one drink is good, two are better?"

I'm sure I have. Isn't that true? And I've also thought that if two are good, three are better. What good is just one or two drinks? Come on, all that proves is that I'm human.

83. Is it true that after your doctor suggested you should stop or cut back on your drinking, you ignored the advice and sought a second opinion?

I did! Then, I got a third and a fourth opinion. The doctor giving me the fourth opinion knew what he was talking about. He said he diagnoses patients with a drinking problem only if they drink more than he does. And since I drink less than him, it's his opinion that I don't have a drinking problem and I don't need to cut back or quit drinking. We can probably save some time if you would just call him.

84. Is it true you have several "rest stops" from your living room to your bed that help you get around easier when you've been drinking?

I wish you would quit listening to her. She's wrong! I don't have "several," just one. She's counting the one between the living room and my bed twice. Now, I'll admit that occasionally, I'll add a rest stop to confuse her.

But, hey, doesn't everybody have a rest stop they use at times? If not, they just don't drink enough—it's that simple.

85. Have you ever thought that your drinking might be causing problems in your life?

Well, I'll admit right now that I'm not a perfect drinker. But at least I'm getting better at it the more I practice. What more can anyone ask for, right?

And no, my drinking doesn't cause my problems. If anything, my problems cause my drinking, and drinking helps me deal with my problems.

86. Have you ever thought or said,
    "I'm not an alcoholic; I don't have
    to drink every day. It's just that I
    don't want to stop once I start?"

Well, I might have said that back when
I didn't drink every day. And even if I
said, "I don't *want* to stop," I didn't say
I *can't* or *don't* stop. There's a difference, you know.

87. Has anyone ever given you a choice: "Either me or drinking?" If so, what did you say or do?

Oh, sure, Sue has. And each time she's said it, I told her, "You win; it's you," and then I hid my drinking until she lightened up. And a time or two when I was able to get *her* drunk, I asked her over and over, "Who's got the problem, now . . . honey?"

88. I understand that you were ex-
pelled from your second DUI
school for asking the teacher if she
could give the class a few tips on
driving drunk without getting
caught. Any comment?

Well, since it was a DUI class, all I
heard about were the dangers of driving
drunk. So, since we all know about that,
I thought a couple of bonus tips would
make it less boring. The teacher said it
wasn't funny, and when I said I was serious, she asked me to leave the class.
Can you believe it?

89. Are you able to quit drinking easily?

I don't know since I've never tried because I've never needed to. But again, this question would be like me asking if you could quit using your smartphone easily. You see, it depends on how you look at things.

90. On an average day, when you have at least one drink, how many do you usually have?

I don't have average days, and I don't count drinks. At least that's one problem I don't have—please note that. I just drink to relax, so I don't quit relaxing to count drinks, especially since Sue counts them for me—if you know what I mean.

Now, sometimes, out of curiosity, I'll keep a rough count if I'm comparing my drinking to someone who's drinking more just to see how they're holding their liquor. Sue should see them, and then she'd know I don't have a drinking problem.

91. Do you feel more knowledgeable after a few drinks?

Well, I'll admit that after a few, my mind releases a flood of knowledge, and then I often feel generous enough to flood everyone else with it. Just one more benefit of drinking.

92. Do you believe drinking alcohol improves your self-image?

Funny, you should ask. Just the other day, I was in this bar and caught a glimpse of myself in the mirror and thought I was looking better by the minute. I don't think about it when I'm not drinking. So, I was convinced that alcohol helps me see the real me, which improves my self-image if that's what you're asking.

93. Do you often feel anger or resentment towards anyone before you start drinking?

Yes, and not only before I drink but also during and after I drink. It's the best way to drink.

94. I've heard that after drinking recently, you attached a crown to
your cat's head, dyed his fur pur-
ple, and called him "King Crown
Royal." Is any of that true?

Everything Sue said was taken out of
context. See, I got this great idea as a
marketing gimmick: *The Purr-fect
Drink.* I was just being creative. When
a neighbor I dislike saw him walking
around dressed up, he reported it. By
the way, here's a picture of Purr-fect!
But he usually looks happier than he
looks in this picture.

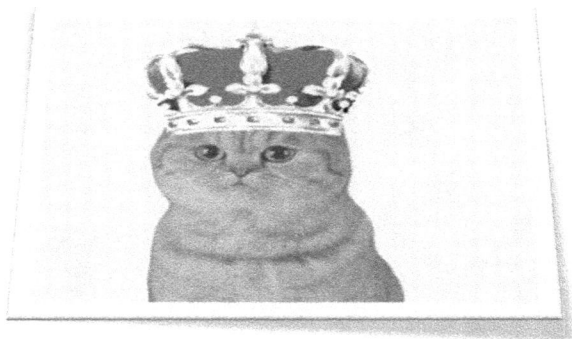

> 95. Have you ever made a New Year's resolution to stop or slow down your drinking? If so, how often, why, and did it work?

Well, of course. I do it every year because everyone does it—it's a New Year's tradition. It doesn't matter if we have a drinking problem or even if we keep the resolution because no one does. Just making it is what matters.

And yes, it worked last New Year's Day. I didn't start drinking until noon *after* Sue and her family had their *one* traditional glass of champagne. I know because they never finish their glasses, so that's my job. And if she told you I didn't wake up until noon, she's lying.

96. Have you ever hidden alcohol in something like a Coke® can?

I can only imagine what she said. Okay, once I took a Coke can filled with liquor to my daughter's Girl Scout event. Come on, everyone's done it. I thought it was no big deal until my daughter asked for a sip in front of the other parents. Sue made a big deal out of it, saying she was so embarrassed. But I was smooth; I said it was empty, so everyone was clueless.

97. Is it true that when you and Sue were recently at a bar, the bartender wrote "LAST CALL!" on a napkin and set in front of you four hours before the bar closed?

Yes, that's how special I am. He didn't want me to feel rushed to order more drinks when they announced "Last Call." No one else gets that kind of advanced notice.

98. Have you ever googled "alcohol- ism?"

Absolutely not. That's what Sue thinks because whenever she passes by and I'm on the computer, all she sees are ads for alcoholism and treatment centers. I don't know why they always pop up when *I'm* on, but not when *she* is. Something suspicious about that.

99. After drinking a few, do you think other people cause your problems?

Bingo. That's one reason I drink. And I'm shocked that no one else sees it. But I'm not saying all my problems, just most. And after talking with Sue, I think you see that she's the one who causes most of my problems.

> 100. Has anyone ever said anything about your drinking? If yes, what?

People often say good things about my drinking, like "You sure know how to drink" or "You're an impressive drinker." In fact, a friend recently praised me for how well I was able to walk, talk, and drive after drinking so much.

101. Are you drinking earlier in the day compared to a year ago?

Well, it may seem that way to Sue, but I'm not obsessed with time like she is, so I don't keep track of it. Now, I'll tell you I use one of those apps that reminds you when it's time to take a pill, but I use it to remind me when it's time to drink. That way, it's out of my hands. Great idea, isn't it?

102. Do you mostly drink alone?

I wouldn't say mostly, but it's hard to say. By alone, do you mean when Sue locks me out of our bedroom? Anyway, I need more alone time than others, but as I've said, my dog, Whiskey, is always with me. So, I never drink alone.

103. Have you felt satisfied enough when drinking that you switched to a nonalcoholic drink in the past year?

I don't get it. If I'm doing something that's satisfying, why would I stop doing it? Doesn't make any sense.

104. I hear that after you've had a few, you can't answer "I don't know" when anyone asks you a question. True?

Well, remember I mentioned how drinking causes my mind to release a flood of knowledge? So, I can't imagine anyone asking me a question I didn't know the answer to after I've had a few. But if I didn't know—again, which I can't imagine—I would only have to drink a couple more, and then I'd know. Does that answer your question?

105. Have you ever made any rules about your drinking, like never drinking before sunset, not drinking two days in a row, or anything like that to prove you don't have a drinking problem?

Sure, I have, and everyone I know has. But things came up, so I was always bending those rules—if you know what I mean. And finally, after I followed the rules enough to prove I didn't have a drinking problem, I decided they didn't make sense, so why have rules I wasn't following? Plus, Sue makes plenty of rules for me that I have to break since I can't bend them.

106. I heard you were cut off during communion and told never to return. Can you explain?

Yes, but it didn't bother me because Sue had been nagging me to go to church, and I didn't plan on returning.

So, what happened was I was expecting wine, not grape juice. Of course, I was shocked and reacted by spitting some out that got on the priest. I said, "Sorry about that, Father, I was expecting wine, and it was just a reaction. But just think, more of the real wine for you!" I was joking, but he didn't find it funny. So, since I knew he was in denial, I did a quick intervention with him while in the line. Still, I can't blame him for not wanting me back, can you?

> **107.** Do you receive mostly alcohol-related gifts, such as flasks, accessories, clothing with beer or whiskey logos, alcohol, novelty items, and shot glasses?

Yeah, I would agree "mostly" because I'm mostly loved. Except on my last birthday, Sue gave me a book called *The Darkness of Denial ... and the alcoholic mind that* shows on its cover some guy dropping a bottle, so I didn't consider it a gift, although it's "alcohol-related." Does that count?

And you know how stressful gift-giving can be. It takes a lot of time to think of the perfect gift for someone who has everything. So, I like being the guy people say is so easy to shop for.

108. Do you think about drinking more after you've been in an argument?

You bet I do! It gives me a good reason to drink. Like whenever Sue says something stupid about my drinking, the first thing I think about is a drink. And I always enjoy drinking more when I'm irritated than when I'm sad or feeling bad about something. Anybody will tell you that.

109. Is it true you once hired an online public relations firm to change your image as an alcoholic? If so, did it work?

It turned out to be a scam like "Happy Hour." I really hired them to change Sue's image of me, not to change me. Can you believe they said, "Just stop drinking?" So . . . since I don't have a drinking problem, I, of course, declined their advice. Come on now, what kind of crazy advice is "Quit drinking?" So, after I had a couple to think about it, I fired and quit paying them.

110. Do you ever try to recapture the good feelings you once had when drinking? If yes, does it work, and if not, why?

Well, of course, I try. But it doesn't work simply because I don't drink enough, and Sue is always on my ass. Still, I keep trying and refuse to give up because I'm not a quitter.

111. Have you ever hidden a bottle?

Bottle or bottles? Hasn't everyone? And I thought I answered this when you asked me where I keep my alcohol, and I said in my trunk and other places. But I've never hidden one from me. And the reason I hide them is because I never know when Sue will go crazy and pour out all the liquor she finds. So, to avoid having to put up with that, I hide them sometimes. Make sense?

112. Have you ever had difficulty finding a bottle you hid?

Well, of course. People misplace stuff all the time. I'm terrible about losing things. At other times, when Sue finds one of my bottles and doesn't pour it out, she thinks it's funny to hide it. Then I may have difficulty finding it, but I usually do, except when she buries it in the garden. So, does that mean I've got a drinking problem because every so often I can't find a bottle Sue hid?

113. Have you ever hidden anything about your drinking?

The only reason I do is to keep Sue and people like her from ruining my drinking by harping on my ass. So, I only hide things about my drinking when I have a good reason to.

114. Do you usually drink more than those you drink with?

Well, it really depends on who I'm drinking with. When I'm drinking with Sue, I always drink more than she does because she rarely drinks.

And when I'm drinking with other people, I usually have to drink more to catch up with them since I'm a champion at holding my liquor. But I don't count the number of drinks they have because that would be weird.

115. Have you ever been in a physical fight when you've been drinking?

Well, sometimes Sue throws things at me, like bottles and kitchen utensils. And she's become quite good at it since she's had a lot of practice. But my only reaction is doing my best to dodge flying objects because it really hurts when something hits me. Is that what you mean?

116. Have you ever had withdrawals when you quit drinking? If so, have you ever drunk alcohol or taken any other substance to prevent alcohol withdrawal?

Well, I wouldn't know since I've never quit drinking. I think you're talking about Skid Row alcoholics.

117. Do you keep an eye on your drinking to make sure it doesn't get out of hand?

I usually don't need to because Sue does it for me. But I do keep an eye on the drink in my hand to make sure it doesn't get out of my hand—if you know what I mean.

118. Sue told me you've said, "I don't need to drink—I can take it or leave it. I just always choose to take it. That's all!" Is that true?

Yes, it's my choice, not a need, which proves I don't have a drinking problem.

119. Have you ever missed work the morning after drinking?

Seriously? Who hasn't? But it wasn't because of drinking; it was because I felt sick.

But the more I think about it, the answer is *no* because I always made up the missed work, and then it was no longer missed. I think your questions are getting more complicated.

120. Do you ever feel remorseful about your drinking?

Well, I like expressing remorse much more than feeling it. And I express it to Sue when I have a hangover, and she's making it worse by going on and on about nothing. But if I really feel remorseful, I know I've either had a good time or didn't drink enough.

121. I've heard that after a few drinks, you can't pass a mirror without slowing down. True?

No, Sue's the one that slows down—I stop!

122. Do you ever leave an unfinished drink behind?

No, why would I? And Sue never drinks the ones I buy her, so I have to drink them.

> 123. Have you ever felt guilty about your drinking? If so, how did you deal with this guilt?

Oh, I have a time or two until I realized Sue was just guilt-tripping me. Then I felt anger instead of guilt, allowing me to drink guilt-free, which, as I've said, is the best way to drink. You see, I've got this figured out.

> 124. Do you feel annoyed or irritated when anyone mentions your drinking?

Not if it's something like, "I like the way you drink." But I do when Sue complains over and over, "You're having another one?" She could drive anyone crazy.

125. Do you think anyone is too concerned about your drinking?

I think any concern about my drinking *is* being too concerned, especially when it's people like Sue and the people she's brainwashed. But they're the type who always need something to be concerned about to give their life purpose—if you know what I mean.

> 126. Even though you don't think you have a drinking problem, does anyone else, other than Sue, think you do?

I don't know what others "think" because I'm not a good mind-reader. But I'll tell you for sure that anyone who thinks I've got a problem has gotten an earful from Sue. So, how close are we to finishing? Just curious.

> 127. Have you ever given a false answer to any question about your drinking?

Only when I'm joking around with Sue, and of course, I do on New Patient Questionnaires, but they expect that. Oh, and when I'm pulled over, I'll say I had a couple. And the other times when I wasn't truthful, it wasn't about anything too important, so my answer is no.

128. Have you ever told anyone that you don't have a drinking problem? If yes, why?

Obviously, I've told you and Sue I don't. And the reason why is just as obvious—because I don't. Other times, it's just how someone looks at me or their tone of voice. But it's not a problem. And it's definitely not a drinking problem.

129. Do you drink faster, slower, or the same as you did three years ago?

It depends on who I'm drinking with. If Sue is around, I always drink faster. And, if I'm in a hurry, I'll drink faster. And, since I hold my liquor better now than three years ago and better than anyone I know, I drink faster to catch up with them. Other than those times, I drink about the same.

130. Do you ever have grandiose ideas while drinking, like making magnificent plans, dreaming about your impressive future, or imagining you're more important than most?

Yes, isn't that what great people do? But that's tough because only time will tell if my ideas are grandiose. In other words, if my ideas become reality, they were never grandiose, right? So, who knows? But I do know that whatever I touch usually turns to gold, even if Sue and others can't see it.

131. Have you ever been banned
from a bar? If so, what did you
do?

Banned? That sounds awful, like for-
ever. You might say I was suspended ...
indefinitely. But it wasn't my fault.

And what did I do? Well, I consid-
ered it a wake-up call to make some pro-
found changes in my life, so I quickly
found a new bar to delight with my
presence. They love me there.

132. How did you feel when you
     learned the last two bars that
     banned you went out of business
     within a month?

My first thought was, "Damn, one person can make a difference in the world, and that one is me." And I wasn't sad to hear it—if you know what I mean. I also remember saying to myself, "Self, maybe you should open a bar. Just your drinking alone could make it successful."

133. I see here that you once visited a family member and *noticed* every trace of alcohol, mouthwash, vanilla extract, and cooking sherry was missing. Do you know why they would hide those items?

Yeah, can you believe it? And I'm sure the only reason they hid them is because of something Sue said. But they only *thought* they hid them.

134. How do you feel about people who can drink without it causing them problems like DUIs, job losses, relationship difficulties, etc.?

Well, they couldn't do it if they had my home life and were married to someone like Sue, harping about their drinking all the time. So, I feel like they're lucky!

135. After a few drinks, has anyone ever said to you, "Why don't you talk louder and repeat yourself some more?"

I don't know because I don't hear others when I'm talking, but if they've said that, doesn't that just prove they want to listen to what I say? I'm not sure what you're getting at.

136. Has a bartender ever refused to serve you a drink?

Less often than you might think. And it was usually after Sue called and told them to stop serving me, so they worried about getting in trouble because of that law . . . I think it's called the Damnshot Act. But after I mentioned the big tip I planned on giving and promised not to drive, they realized it was just an honest mistake. Now, every time she calls, they just roll their eyes and say, "Your wife called again." It's embarrassing.

137. Have you ever felt like a hopeless failure, but after a few drinks, felt like a huge success?

You bet! Just another benefit of drinking. In fact, once, after listening to Sue ramble on about nothing, I started feeling really down. So, I had a few drinks, and within minutes, I imagined a movie about my greatness.

What an amazing gift it is to have a liquid I can drink that changes my mood in minutes! I think it's clear that drinking is the solution, not the problem.

138. Has your drinking ever resulted in hospitalization or admission to a treatment center?

Nope. And since it hasn't, that should tell you right there that I don't have a drinking problem.

> ## 139. Have you lost any friends because of your drinking?

No, not because of my drinking but because of Sue's attitude. They don't like hanging out because she runs them off by saying things like, "You guys know it's one in the morning, and it's a school night?" or "Could you keep it down a little bit? The kids are sleeping."

Then, some just couldn't keep up with me, so we grew apart. But here's the good news: I replaced them with real friends who understand and appreciate me and drink like I do or more.

140. Have you ever attended a court-ordered alcohol assessment? If so, what was the result?

Yes, and it resulted in me having a few with the evaluator, her taking advantage of me, and giving me a notarized certificate certifying I don't have a drinking problem. I handed it to you before we started.

Come to think of it, John, I need to check the parking meter; do you want to take a break and check it with me? I have a bottle in my trunk, so we could take a shot. Just asking.

> 141. Have you ever waited in a long line to get a drink? If so, how did you feel?

Now, you're testing my patience. Pun intended. I'm cool if I have a drink with me while I'm waiting. But if Sue's with me, it's terrible. She stands on the side with her arms crossed, her eyes shooting daggers and mouthing, "Again?" Then it's a bit tense, but I think I handled it well by ignoring her. Any other questions?

142. I heard that recently, after quite a few drinks, you suddenly felt compelled to express your love for everyone by shouting louder and louder in the ear of the nearest person, repeating yourself over and over while tolerating no interruption, and spraying spit mists every few words because you were too drunk to remember to swallow. Any truth to that?

Okay, I can only imagine what she told you, but the truth is that I'm at this party and meet this guy who asks a complicated question, which I'm kind enough to answer. He's hard of hearing, and it's loud, so I repeat myself over and over while speaking louder and louder. But it's Sue who sprays spit mists when she's shouting at me because she's too pissed off to swallow.

143. I've heard that after having a few, you tend to ponder your brilliance. If so, how often?

Yes, I admit I am a ponderer. Do you have something with sufficient ponderability for me to ponder? This is a long test, and I'm getting a little tired, but I'll try to be serious. Let's see. When I act or think brilliantly, which is often, I ponder my brilliance for a few minutes several times a day. And yes, drinking enhances my ponderations. For example, as part of my pondering, I ponder the ignorant, which helps me ponder my brilliance. In fact, drinking makes everything more ponderable. I hope that answers your question, although it can't tell you anything about my drinking.

> 144. So, I started this session by asking if you've ever wondered if you might have a drinking problem. Has your answer changed?

Yes! I said the only drinking problem I have is when I have a problem getting a drink. But this session has opened my eyes—I now *know* my drinking problem is Sue interfering with my drinking. Can I go now?

145. Well, Jim, I'll tell you what. After this session, I'm ready to check that parking meter with you—if you know what I mean.

Yes, John, I know what you mean! I knew you'd come around. Let's go!

CONTACT INFORMATION

SUICIDE & CRISIS LIFELINE:
Call or text 988 or chat at 988lifeline.org

SUICIDE PREVENTION LIFELINE:
1-800-273-TALK (8255)

For confidential information about help for alcohol dependence, contact one or more of the following:

NIAAA ALCOHOL TREATMENT NAVIGATOR
"Pointing the way to evidence-based care"
A service of the U.S. federal government providing unbiased information for finding quality alcohol treatment through mutual support groups, therapists, doctors, and outpatient & inpatient care.
www.alcoholtreatment.niaaa.nih.gov

—

MUTUAL-SUPPORT GROUPS

(AA) Alcoholics Anonymous
www.aa.org | 212–870–3400
(or local phone directory)

Al-Anon Family Services/Alateen
For Those Affected by Another's Drinking
www.al-anon.org | 888-425-2666 for meetings

Adult Children of Alcoholics & Dysfunctional Families
www.adultchildren.org | 310–534–1815

AA Agnostica
A space for AA agnostics, atheists and freethinkers worldwide
www.aaagnostica.org | admin@aaagnostica.org.

Celebrate Recovery
A Christ-Centered Recovery Program
www.celebraterecovery.com | 800-723-3532

LifeRing
Secular (nonreligious) Recovery
www.LifeRing.org | 800-811-4142

Moderation Management
www.moderation.org | 212–871–0974

Secular Organizations for Sobriety
www.sossobriety.org | 314-353–-3532

Secular Alcoholics Anonymous
AA meetings for agnostics, atheists and freethinkers
www.secularaa.org

SMART Recovery
An Alternative to AA, Al-Anon, and other 12-Step Programs
www.smartrecovery.org | 440-951-5357

Women for Sobriety
www.womenforsobriety.org | 215–536–8026

INFORMATION RESOURCES

The Alcohol and Drug Addiction Resource Center
(800) 390-4056

Alcohol and Drug Helpline
www.alcoholanddrughelpline.com | (800) 821-4357

Alcohol Hotline Support & Information
(800) 331-2900

American Council on Alcoholism (ACA)
www.recoverymonth.gov | (800) 527-5344

National Child Abuse Hotline
1-800-25-ABUSE

National Clearinghouse for Alcohol and Drug Information
www.ncadi.samhsa.gov | (800) 729–6686

National Council on Alcoholism & Drug Dependence, Inc.
www.ncadd.org | *HOPE LINE*: 800/NCA-CALL (24-hour)

National Domestic Abuse Hotline
1-800-799-SAFE

National Helpline
Treatment referral and information 24-7
www.samhsa.gov | 1-800-662-HELP (4357)

National Institute on Alcohol Abuse and Alcoholism
www.niaaa.nih.gov | (301) 443–3860

National Institute on Drug Abuse
www.nida.nih.gov | (301) 443–1124

National Institute of Mental Health
www.nimh.nih.gov | (866) 615–6464

www.ingramcontent.com/pod-product-compliance
Lightning Source LLC
Chambersburg PA
CBHW071451070426
42452CB00039B/1032